LOVE
Breathes With Me

A Book of Poems & Prayers

Cathy AJ Hardy

◆ FriesenPress

Suite 300 - 990 Fort St
Victoria, BC, V8V 3K2
Canada

www.friesenpress.com

Copyright © 2018 by Cathy AJ Hardy
First Edition — 2018

All rights reserved.

No part of this publication may be reproduced in any form, or by any means, electronic or mechanical, including photocopying, recording, or any information browsing, storage, or retrieval system, without permission in writing from FriesenPress.

ISBN
978-1-5255-1764-8 (Hardcover)
978-1-5255-1765-5 (Paperback)
978-1-5255-1766-2 (eBook)

1. POETRY

Distributed to the trade by The Ingram Book Company

Table of Contents

Eternal Love	1
Prayer of Aligning with Love	2
I Bind My Life to Love	4
Dancing Alone	5
Transformation	7
Life Dances	10
O My Soul	12
Surrender	14
Advent Prayer	16
Lenten Journey – 40 Days	18
Monday Evening Prayer	24
Tuesday Evening Prayer	25
Wednesday Evening Prayer	26
Thursday Evening Prayer	27
Friday Evening Prayer	28
Saturday Evening Prayer	30
Sunday Evening Prayer	32
All is Beauty	34
Begin Again	36
Dare to Trust	38
Birthing Me	40
Prayer Journey (Lord's Prayer)	43
With You	44
Ebb & Flow	47
Arms of Grace	52
One Soul	54
Love Breathes with Me	55
The Chalice	56

*Enclosed in this book are
prayers and poetry of
my heart from the past twenty years.*

*May they be a gift of light, life & love
for your soul.*

Love, Cathy

Eternal Love

Eternal Love
Encircling...eternally
Where can I go
Where Love is not?
Though I may not see
I may not hear
I may not be aware...

Tender breath
Wild winds
Raging fire
Silent stars
Reflect the mystery

That surrounds
Enfolds
Sustains
Infuses
Every moment
Eternal Love
Encircling...eternally

Prayer of Aligning with Love

May my bones shine with the radiance of the
Presence of Love
May my heart beat with the joy of knowing
my intrinsic value
May my mind be filled with thoughts and
intentions rooted in the
Creator's love for me
May my longings align with
Love's longings
May my feet be carried to
where I need to be
May my eyes behold beauty
May my mouth speak truth
May my hands be open and receptive to
all Love longs to give

May my hands offer blessing
to all they touch
May I move out of Love's response
rather than fear's reaction
May I be energized by Love
May I receive forgiveness and compassion
May I offer forgiveness and compassion
May I receive grace and mercy
May I offer grace and mercy
May I receive the gaze of Love
May I become the reflection of the
gaze of Love
May I become the radiance of the
Presence of Love

I Bind My Life to Love

I bind my mind to Love

I bind my heart to Love

I bind my feet

To the path Love has for me

I bind my hands

To receive the blessing

Of the fullness of Life

I bind my hands

To bless all I touch

I bind my life to Love

Dancing Alone

Longing for connection
I look for old,
familiar ways
But they are gone

Reaching back my hand
To hang onto something sure
But there is
Only moonlight

Dancing alone
In the moonlight
Stars in the universe
Sway with me

Dancing alone
In the moonlight
I am in
Great company

6 ~ *Cathy AJ Hardy*

Transformation

I breathe in the sky
I breathe out
I breathe in the light
I breathe out
I breathe in the trees
I breathe out
I breathe in the field
I breathe out
I breathe in the rocky cliff
I breathe out
I breathe in the river flow
I breathe out
I breathe in LIFE
I breathe out transformation

I breathe in eagle's wings
I breathe out
I breathe in the rain
I breathe out
I breathe in the wind
I breathe out
I breathe in stardust
I breathe out
I breathe in the curve of the moon
I breathe out
I breathe in sunlight
I breathe out
I breathe in LIFE
I breathe out transformation

Love Breathes With Me ~ 9

Life Dances

A coming to a close
a turning of the page
the past will always
be
inside of me
and yet
it doesn't have to
have a
hold
on me
life dances
with
a constant interaction
of the mystery
of what is seen
with the
mystery of
what is unseen
a tapestry of moments
meetings
infinite
possibilities

Let me be gentle
with the pages
already turned

Let me be open
to a new chapter of living

Let me know the adventure
of a story
not yet complete

O My Soul

O my soul
Be not afraid
O my soul
Be not afraid

Let not the terrors of suffering
And the overwhelm of the world
Cause you to lose heart
Breathe

Breathe
Open
Open

Allow
Love
To whisper truth
To your inner being

Receive
Receive
O my soul

And in receiving
May you be transformed
By grace

And become a bearer
Of this grace

Be still
Be still

Awaken
Awaken
O my soul

Surrender

Pause
Wait
Not sure of where to
Place my step

Pause
Wait
I've never travelled
Here before

More uncertainty
Than clarity to my thoughts
All I have
Are questions
And my questions
Are my prayer

My hands are reaching
For something I can grasp
My feet are yearning
For a firm
Foundation

In all unknowing
I
am
here

I place my heart
in the light of the sun
I place my hands
on the quest of my heart
I place my feet
in the path of this quest
and
Surrender

Advent Prayer

Advent is a season
of waiting, of longing, of active
attentiveness to what is being birthed.
Advent is a time of pregnancy,
of expectation,
of yearning
for the reality of Love's presence
within us and in the whole world.

Advent is a time
of being present to the darkness
of the womb during pregnancy;
of being present to the unknown,
to mystery, to what is yet unseen
and still being formed.

Advent is a time
of trusting in the midst
of whatever darkness we are in,
trusting as Mary did that
light would emerge for the path ahead.

Advent invites us to open our hearts,
to trust amidst darkness,
and make room
for Love;
Love with Us
and
Love Birthing within Us.

This longing is made up of simplicity,
of expectancy,
of hope
and the
spirit of childhood and joy.

Lenten Journey – 40 Days

When I spent 40 days in the desert
And wondered if I was losing my mind
And perhaps, in some moments, I did
Rational thought
Seemed far away
A distant memory
Survival
Desperation
Longing
Loneliness beyond understanding
Bone-ripping pain

No facilities for care
It is wild
It is a wild journey
Of the soul
Quaking from the
Cellular level

A death occurred
A death of myself
And I surrendered to this death
A profound letting go
Of all I knew

Of safety
Security
Known sign posts
All gone
Gone

Left barren
Disoriented

Till
Dead
Dead in the dry wild
Air
Of the desert
Night
Silence
Stillness

Then
To my crazed mind
I found my heart
Was still beating
Or did it return to beating?
Where does death end
And living begin?
The lines are blurred

And so with mud-caked skin
Wild hair
Torn nails
Bleeding palms
Crawling in the sand
I landed

In a new place
And the sound
Of singing
The sound of cheers
Are baffling

Have they been with me all along?
I thought I was alone
But they were there
Calling to me

To carry on
Keep walking
Crawling
Being

And the song
Begins to fill me
Cell by cell
Until

All
Are vibrating
And transforming
From the centre
Outwards

I'm alive
I'm alive
I'm alive

Love Breathes With Me

Daily Evening Prayers

Monday Evening Prayer

Around each corner
Is a new opportunity
To let go
Of what we were expecting
To let go
Of how we thought
Life might be
And to say 'yes'
To this
Place
Here and now
This new beginning
Just as we are...
Just as things are...
And in this place
This day
This moment
We say
Yes
To trusting
To Love within and all around
Yes
For this
New beginning

Tuesday Evening Prayer

O Beloved, You breathe new life in us for each new day.
May we awaken to Your breath within us.

Source of Life, You fill all the earth with the vibrancy of creation.
May we awaken to what You are birthing in us.

Compassionate Heart, You are present in our deepest darkness.
May we awaken to Your love in the midst of our pain.

Redeeming Healer, You restore our wounded hearts.
May we awaken to the grace of transformation.

Beautiful Presence, You bring hope when we are weary.
May we awaken to what is possible in the
midst of the impossible.

Radiant Light, You enter our night and illumine the way.
May we awaken to Your guidance and leading.

Wednesday Evening Prayer

Creator
Life-bearer
Breathing Life of All
Beloved
Friend
Bearer of Grace
I open my heart, I open my heart
To You, O Heart of my heart
How I love You
How I love You
How I love You

Thursday Evening Prayer

You are the one who dwells in us
You are our rest
You are the one who takes down walls
You are our peace
You are the one who reconciles
You are our joy
You are the one inviting us
To come to the table

You encircle
And invite us to encircle others
And all of life.

We open to You
You are the fulfillment of our longings, cries and hopes
We say YES to your Presence
O Encircling Love

Thank you
Thank you
Thank you

Love Breathes With Me

Friday Evening Prayer

O Divine Love
We open our hearts to You.
You see the vastness of our souls
and the areas we need to let go of
so we can abide in You.

Restore our wounded hearts.
Guide us into deeper truth.
Liberate us into a life of joy;
Reflecting Your beauty, mercy and kindness.

We let go of anxiety
...and say yes to resting in Love
We let go of our desire to control our lives
...and say yes to surrendering to the path
We let go of fear
... and say yes to trusting even in obscurity
We let go of striving
...and say yes to moving in the flow of grace
We let go of heaviness
...and say yes to Love's never-ending abundance
We let go of shame
...and say yes to our true value and dignity;
for ourselves, for others, and for all of creation
We let go of our blindness to Love's Presence
...and say yes to looking for Love in the ordinary and
naming those places Holy Ground

Saturday Evening Prayer

God of Companionship
Thank You for Your steadfast friendship in our lives
Even in our dark nights
When we are unaware of Your loving Presence
Open our hearts to greater trust

God of Compassion
Thank You for your profound outpouring of love
Even when we are blind to it
Open our hearts to greater receptivity

God of Mercy
Thank You for your ever-flowing grace towards us
Releasing us from shame and offering tenderness
Open our hearts to your kindness

God of Restoration
Thank You that you come
To seek and to restore all that is lost
Open our hearts to fulfill Your healing work in our lives

God of Justice
Thank You that You desire 'Shalom' for all
Open our hearts to align
With Your passion for every human being and all of creation

God of Abundance
Thank You that you invite us to the table
To know fellowship with you now and forever
Open our hearts in greater ways to the mystery of this communion

Sunday Evening Prayer

May our hearts come to stillness
May our bodies come to rest
May our eyes see the mystery
May our ears hear the whispers
May our hands receive the gifts
May our souls navigate the depths
to the well-springs of joy
May we drink deeply and may our whole beings
Be
Renewed
Revived
Restored
Returned
Home

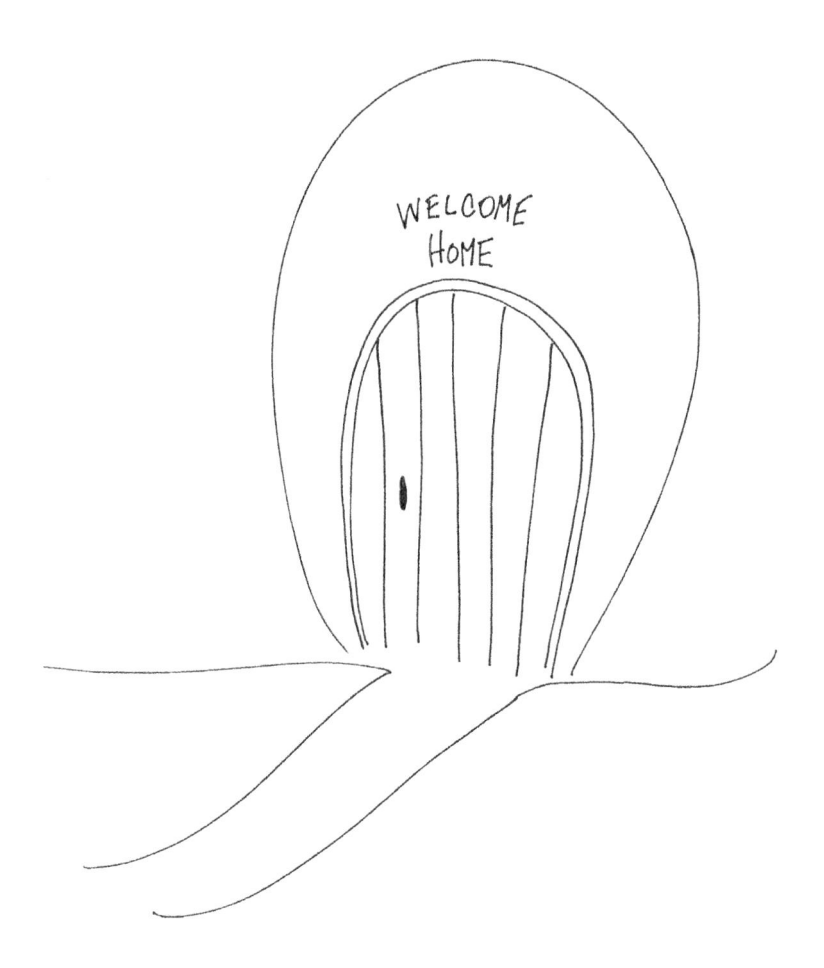

All is Beauty

You stand on the edge
Of the unknown
Preparing your heart
For travelling home

What is in shadow
For you will be clear
Your new tomorrow
So far, yet so near

May Love surround you
As you depart
May Love surround you
And carry your heart

To the Great Beauty
That we call home
You're going to Beauty
And soon you will know

All is well
All is well
All is beauty

All is well
All is beauty
All is well

Begin Again

Begin
Again
Fresh
New
Light
Open
Doors
Winged
Opportunities
Fly
High
Soar
Alert
Attentive
Meeting
Possibilities
Welcoming
Surprises
Awaiting
Goodness

Beauty
Surrounds
Beauty
Free
Eyes
Clear
Heart
Clean
Hands
Lifted
Ears
Listening
Spirit
Aware
Awake
Alive
Love
Love
Between
Me and you

Love
Between
Me and all
I touch
See
Know
Love
Unfolds
Breathing
Deeply
Breathing
Fully
Breathing
Consciously
I
Am
Here
I
Embrace
What

Love
Brings
Yes
To
Goodness
Fruitfulness
Well-being
Peace
Wisdom
Provision
Protection
Fulfillment
The
Centre
Of
My
Being
Love
Born
Again

Dare to Trust

It has been hard to say
    'I did what I could'
when that means
      that I have to admit
        that I can't hold
      everything
     together
       all the time
to allow
  things
to fall and crash and break
    to allow
  things
    to get lost and not found
       to allow
  misperceptions to be without freaking
to allow
  my carefully laid plans to
fall apart
to allow
    the feeling of emptiness
      to come close to me
        when I feel that things are slipping
through my fingers

to allow
> my heart
>> to say
>>> YES
>>>> To You

In the midst of these moments
> And not lose heart

To be willing to be turned
> Upside down
>> And shaken

Loose
> Of my firm grip
>> On things

So I can rest
> In my poverty
>> And humanity

And dare to trust
> In your abundance
>> And divinity

And then celebrate the mystery
> The paradox
>> The miracle

Of Emmanuel
> You within and all around

Birthing Me

I twist and turn
Not knowing
That I am in You
I kick and wave my arms
Not knowing
That You surround me

At times I am
Aware
Of a rhythm
Of a flow
A beating of
A Great Heart
At times I am
Aware
Of a rush
Of Love
Flowing in these waters

Even so, I am in darkness
And unable to touch You

At times
I am lost
In this sea of becoming
And I don't
Yet
Know
That You
Are birthing
Me

Love's One Desire

Prayer Journey (Lord's Prayer)

Inspired by the Aramaic translation work of Neil Douglas- Klotz

Creator, Radiant Love, Breathing Life of All

Your name, Your name lives within my soul

May Love reign here, may Love reign in me

Love's one desire,
Love's one desire unite with ours

Grant us what we need,
Grant us what we need today

Release us, release us from our shame

As we forgive, as we forgive too

Liberate us, liberate us in the way of Love

Glory and beauty, radiant harmony,
Love's eternal song shall sing on

Amen, amen, amen

With You

I feel your pain, my friend
I feel the shards of your being
As you have so honestly
Opened up
The shadow places of your life
Places before speech developed
Childhood echoes of
Being silenced
And abandoned
And you are waking up to the reality that they still live
In some ancient
Memory of your cells
And I feel this with you
Right now
Even though we are apart
There is an awareness of
Your story
Your heart
Your shards
Rough edges that rub against the
Smooth of the day
And make you bleed
I feel this with you
In this moment
Even though I don't know if

You can feel me
I ask you to look
Look up and see me there
Before you
Look in my eyes
There is no part of you
That is too much for me
There is no pain that I cannot sit
With together with you
There is no shame you carry that I
Cannot be with
Together, can we be with these
Shards?
Together, can you
Let me hold you?
Even now
Across these miles
Surrounding you, beyond me
Is a radius of light
And warmth
And beauty
This Great Love
Knows all of your suffering
And also knows your true name
Let the Great Love closer
My friend

Become aware as the Great Love
Baptizes you with tender touches
Of healing
I see it happening
The beauty being poured down
Your forehead and into your soul
Flowing to all your cells
Each one receiving grace in this
Moment
Being kissed
You are kissed with the
Great Love

I love you and all that you are
How alone you have felt for so
Much of your life
Yet you have dared
To open
To beauty
To trust
To journey
May your heart receive all it needs
In this moment
Even though you can't see me
I am
With you

Ebb & Flow

As I stand on the shore of change
I feel the ebb and flow
Of the tides

The energy of
The ocean
Moving towards me
Life
Beauty
Laughter
Washing over me

And then
I am aware of sand sinking
Beneath
My feet
The sucking of life
Pulling away from me
As the water retreats
And I am left
Barren
On the shore
In pools of grief

Letting go of what was
Familiar
And present to my
Unknown future
I am reminded
Of a time past

When I saw myself as a tree
And the beautiful gardener
Came to me
With tender eyes
But an axe
In his hand
And he chopped
All my branches off
Till I was only a stump
I was a stump for a long time

What I had thought
Was important
Needed to be pruned
Away
And little did I know
That roots needed time
To grow
Deep down into the earth
So that my tree could
Come back to life

I was very surprised one day
When I realized
I was growing again
New life
Coming back
New branches
Being formed

And the tree was now more solid
Than it had ever been
And the roots have continued
To grow

There has been an
Ebb and flow
To my tree

Times of growth
Times of deepening
Times of fruit bearing
And times of letting the leaves fall

And now I must trust
That these deep roots
Are even deeper
Than the ebb and flow
Of the ocean waters
That come
Close to me

My humanity
Longs for certainty
For predictability
For normalcy

My prayer
Is that my heart can remain
Open
To trusting
To loving
To resting
To being

In the midst of the ebb and flow
That I may embrace
The moments that are full
And wash over me
With abundance

And that I may let the tears flow
When the tides of emptiness
And longing
Pull the waters back again
Into the wide ocean
Knowing that my roots
Are tapped
Into streams of living water
And I will
Live

Love Breathes With Me

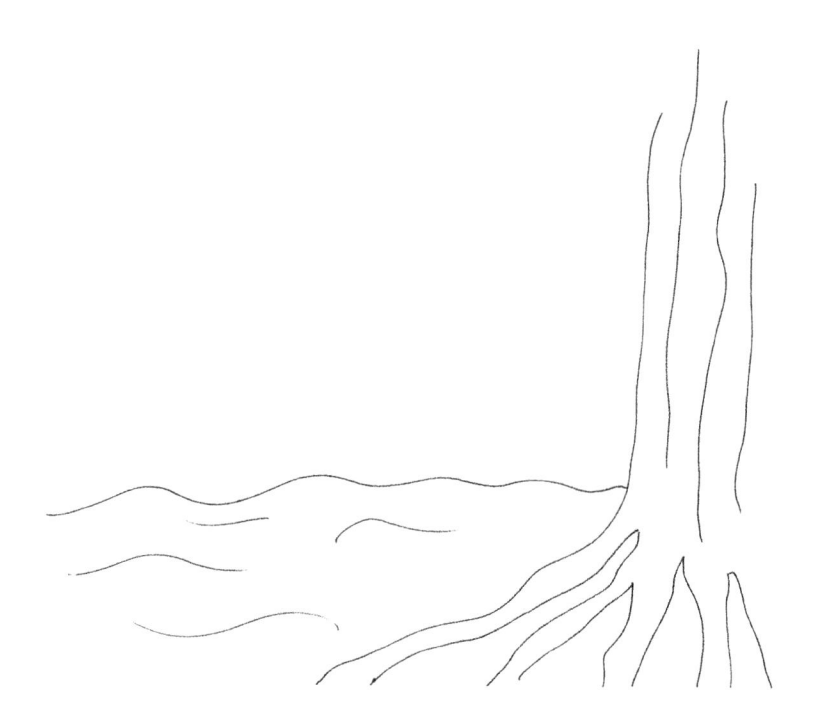

Arms of Grace

I am welcomed
In these arms
Even when I
Do not understand
How great this Love is
That welcomes me

I had understood
This Love had limitations
I understood
It had judgments
I understood
It abandoned me
I understood
It betrayed me

I was wrong.

I never knew

How wide
How deep
How high
How wild
How fierce
How passionate
Is the Love
In which we are held
Every moment
Every hour
Every day

Even
When
We
Do
Not
Know

Love Breathes With Me ~ 53

One Soul

One soul
Is a universe
When you open
The door of your heart
I see galaxies of star travel
To explore
I hear the explosion of
Waterfalls of grandeur
And the silence of
Deep-growth forests
I feel the expanse of wide-open
Vistas for me to walk gently on
For the path is your very heart
And in this moment
Of trust
You opened
A door
And allowed me
To enter

Love Breathes with Me

Tears
Can't breathe
I can't breathe
The pain in my chest overwhelms
All ability to function
But then You are there
Where did You come from?
Silently
Present
To me
And without words
Without fanfare
Without shame or condemnation
Without restraint
Without blame
Without judgment
You breathed *with* me
Until once again
I began to live

The Chalice

I am the cup
For Love to fill
I receive
And am transformed

Pour me out
Let Love abound
And spread from
Shore to shore
Let Love abound

Let Love abound
Let Love abound
Once more

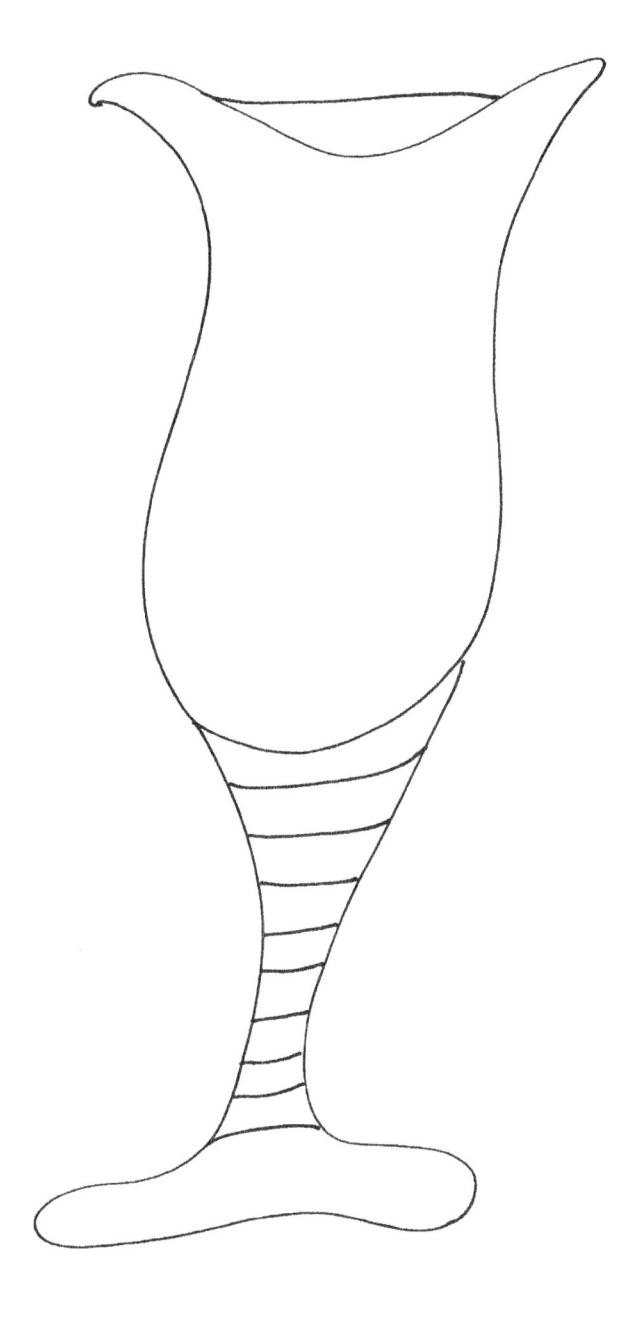

Love Breathes With Me ~ 57

CPSIA information can be obtained
at www.ICGtesting.com
Printed in the USA
LVOW03s0406150218
566591LV00004B/4/P

9 781525 517655